Art's Alive!

What are Textiles?

Ruth Thomson

W

FRANKLIN WATTS
LONDON•SYDNEY

First published in 2004 by Franklin Watts
338 Euston Road, London NW1 3BH

Franklin Watts Australia, Hachette Children's Books
Level 17/207 Kent Street, Sydney NSW 2000

© Franklin Watts 2004

Editor: Caryn Jenner
Design: Sphere Design
Art director: Jonathan Hair
Picture research: Diana Morris
Art consultant: Janet Pope

The publisher wishes to thank Fiona Cole for her assistance with the artwork and activities in this book.
Thanks also to Florence McLaughlin and Heather Webster.

All photographs taken by Ray Moller unless otherwise credited.

Acknowledgements:
With special authorisation of the City of Bayeux/Bridgeman Art Library: 17. Dinodia: 19. DPA/The Image Works/Topham: 22tl. Pascal Goetgheluck/SPL: 9br. Historical Picture Archive/Corbis: 23. Jeremy Horner/Corbis: 15. Wolfgang Kaehler/Corbis: 21. Kelley-Mooney Photography/Corbis: 13. Lawrence Manning/Corbis: 10cr. Philadephia Museum of Art/Corbis: front cover, 25. Anders Ryman/Corbis: 10cl. Joseph Sohm, ChromoSohm Inc./Corbis: 9tl. Adam Woolfitt/Corbis: 8bl.

Every attempt has been made to clear copyright. Should there be any inadvertent omission please apply to the publisher for rectification.

A CIP catalogue record for this book is available from the British Library

ISBN 978 0 7496 7356 7

Printed in China

Franklin Watts is a division of Hachette Children's Books.

Contents

What are textiles?

Textiles are made from **fibres**. Other words for textiles are cloth, material and fabric.

Clothes ▶

Clothes are made from soft, comfortable textiles. They trap air to keep us warm.

◀ Towels

Some textiles soak up water easily. We use them to dry ourselves after a wash or bath.

Bags ▶

Some textiles are tough and waterproof. They are perfect for making backpacks.

How many different textiles can you see in this picture?

A textile hunt
Look around your home to see how many different textiles you can find. Search in the bathroom and kitchen, and in cupboards and drawers.

What are textiles made from?

Some textiles, such as wool, cotton and silk, are made from **natural** fibres.

Wool keeps you warm.

◀ **Wool**
Wool comes from sheep. Farmers clip the wool off the sheep. The sheep will soon grow more!

What does it feel like?
Feel some textiles. What are they like? Use these words to help describe them.

soft   warm   scratchy
rough   heavy   light
slippery   smooth   fluffy

Cotton

Cotton comes from the seed-hairs of a plant. The seed pods are called bolls. Each one has thousands of hairs.

Cotton keeps you cool.

Silk

Silk comes from the cocoons of silkworms. Workers unravel long silk threads from the cocoons and twist them together.

Silk is soft and light.

Making yarn

The fibres of wool or cotton are twisted together into long lengths of **yarn**. This is called spinning.

▲ Hand-spinning
This woman twirls a **spindle** and pulls the wool. The fibres get longer and twist together to make yarn.

▲ Hand-dyeing
Dye gives the yarn colour. Here, yarn is being coloured in a pot of blue dye.

Look at the labels inside your clothes to see what they are made of.

◀ ▲ **Machine-made**
Most wool and cotton is spun and dyed in factories called mills. Mills also make yarns that are not natural, such as viscose and acrylic.

▲ **Knitting wool**
Wool like this is often used for knitting.

Twisting yarn
Roll a piece of cotton wool between your hands. See how the fibres lengthen as you twist them together.

Weaving

Cloth is made by criss-crossing threads over and under each other on a frame called a **loom**. This is known as weaving.

Warp and weft ▶

Look at some woven cloth. Threads that go up and down are called the warp. Threads that go across are called the weft.

Weaving with paper

warp —　　　— weft

1 Lay paper strips lengthwise on card, leaving spaces in between. Glue both ends on to the card.

2 Cut more strips in other colours. Weave one strip over and under the warp strips.

3 Weave the next strip *under* and then *over*. Repeat steps 2 and 3 until your weaving is complete.

shuttle with weft
thread wound inside

warp threads

🔺 Weaving

This woman is weaving on a big
wooden loom. She is about to put the
shuttle through the warp threads to
make the criss-crossing weft threads.

Weaving patterns

Textiles with coloured **patterns** are made when the warp and weft threads are different colours.

▲ **Patterned cloth**
Patterns on modern looms are computer-controlled. The patterns can be very simple or very complicated.

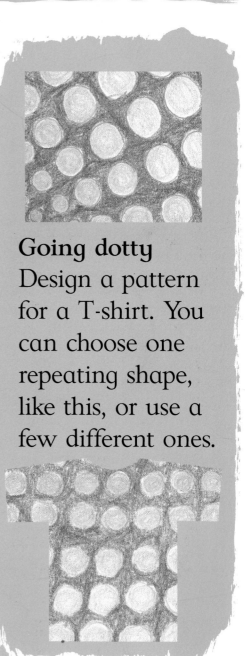

Going dotty
Design a pattern for a T-shirt. You can choose one repeating shape, like this, or use a few different ones.

What three animals can you see in the pattern of this textile?

▲ Tarabuco weaving from South America

This textile was woven by hand. The weaver used several shuttles with different coloured threads to make these patterns.

Embroidery

Embroidery is a way of decorating textiles with stitched patterns or pictures.

Fancy fish ▶
This embroidery was made with smooth, silky threads.

A glittery bag ▲
Sequins and beads can be added to embroideries.

A thread picture
Draw an outline picture on stiff card. Glue some embroidery threads over the outlines.

▲ The Bayeux Tapestry

This long, woollen embroidery was made more than 900 years ago. It tells the story of how William the Conqueror and his men sailed from France to England, and won the Battle of Hastings in 1066.

Tie-and-dye

If some parts of a textile are tied before it is dyed, these parts do not change colour.

1 See for yourself by tie-dying a white T-shirt. Ask a grown-up to help you.

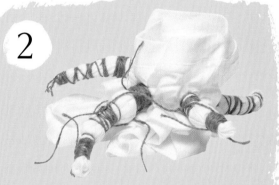

2 Bunch up parts of the T-shirt and tie them tightly with thread, like this.

3 Ask a grown-up to soak the T-shirt in dye. Rinse it well and leave it to dry.

4 Untie the threads. The T-shirt will have white patches where it was tied.

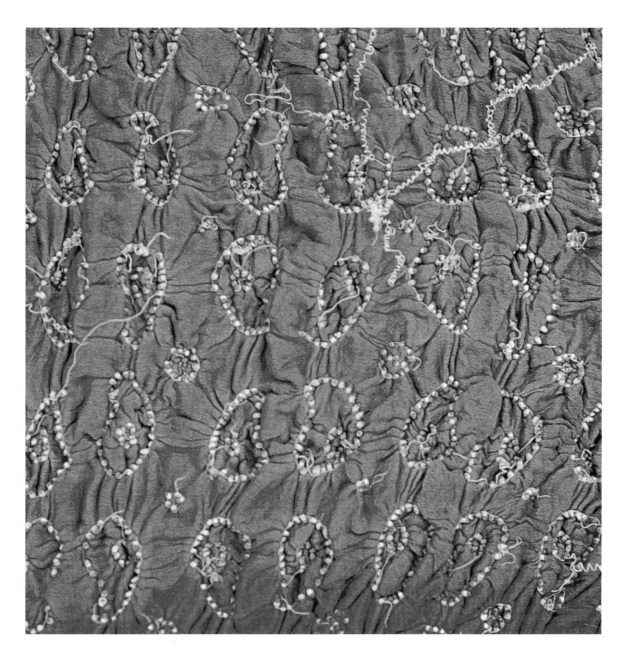

▲ Tie-dyed cloth from India

Look how many bunches have been tied
in this textile. The cloth has been dyed,
but the threads have not yet been untied.

Batik

To make batik, people draw patterns on textiles using a pen of hot wax. Then they dye the textiles. The dye does not stick to wax.

Hand-drawn patterns
When the wax is removed, the pattern shows up on the undyed cloth.

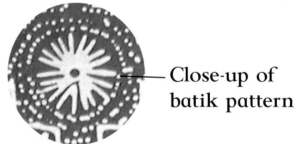

Close-up of batik pattern

A waxy picture
Using wax crayons, draw a pattern on some paper. Paint over it with watery paint. The wax marks will show through the paint.

▲ Fish batik from Indonesia

This batik was waxed and dyed many times, starting with the lightest colour and ending with the darkest. Some colours mixed together to make new colours.

Look carefully at this batik. In what order do you think the colours were dyed?

Block printing

Another way to make patterns on textiles is by printing with wood blocks.

sponge blocks

▲ Repeating patterns

The printer presses an inky block on to cloth again and again to make a pattern.

Sponge prints

Cut some sponges into shapes. Dip them in paint. Press them on to paper to make a printed picture.

carved wood blocks

What animals can you see hiding among the plants?

▲ **Brother Rabbit print,
William Morris, 1882**

This cloth is printed with a pattern
of leaves, flowers and animals.

Patchwork

Patchwork is usually made from many different-coloured pieces of cloth.

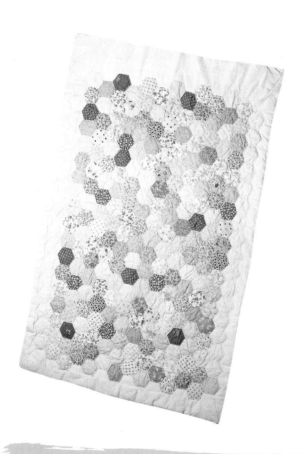

 Patchwork pieces
Long ago, women saved scraps left over from dress-making. They cut these into shapes and sewed them together to make patchwork **quilts** like this one.

Common patchwork shapes

square   diamond   hexagon

Patchwork patterns
Carefully colour squared paper to make lots of different patchwork patterns.

Can you see what shape has been used to make this starry quilt?

🔺 **Patchwork quilt,
Rebecca Scattergood Savery, 1839**

A patchwork quilt like this takes a long time to make. Sometimes, a group of people get together to sew a quilt. This is called a quilting bee.

Appliqué

Appliqué pictures have layers of fabric.
The layers are stitched one on top of the other.

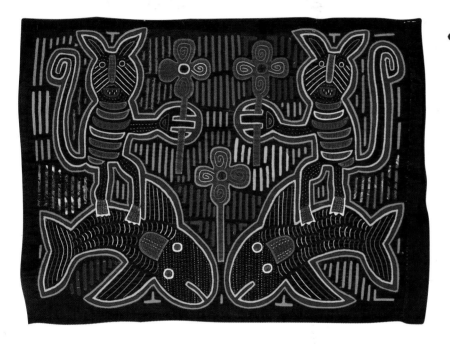

Crazy cats

This picture has many layers of fabric. The black layer is on top. It has been cut away to let the other colours show through.

A whale of a time
Make your own appliqué picture. Cut some fabric shapes and glue them to a piece of stiff card.

How many different animals, birds and insects can you spot below?

◀ Appliqué from Colombia

This colourful appliqué shows everyday country life in Colombia, South America. What are all the people doing?

Quiz

1. Find three things in the book that are made from textiles and can be used to carry things.

2. Does wool come from a plant or animal?

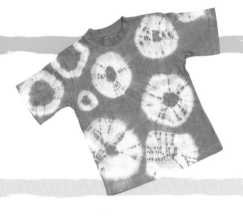

3. Has this T-shirt been dyed or printed?

4. What is this used for?

5. What is the name for textiles made with layers of cloth?

Glossary

dye A dye is used to change the colour of textiles. The textiles are usually soaked or dipped in dye.

fibre A very thin thread. Fibres are twisted together to make yarn.

loom A machine used to weave yarn into cloth.

natural Found in nature. Wool, cotton and silk are examples of natural textiles.

pattern A repeated design.

quilt A cover for a bed. Quilts are often made with patchwork.

shuttle A tool used with a weaving loom. The shuttle holds the weft thread as it criss-crosses with the warp threads to make cloth.

spindle A thin rod used to spin yarn.

yarn Thread used for making cloth. Yarn is made from fibres such as wool, cotton or silk.

Websites

www.crayola.com
A colourful site with lots of fabric craft ideas and activities.

www.bayeuxtapestry.org.uk
An explanation of the story depicted in the Bayeux Tapestry and information on the history of the Tapestry itself.

www.americanhistory.si.edu/quilts/
Pictures of all sorts of quilts, including patchwork, appliqué and embroidery.

www.morrissociety.org
A website about the life and work of William Morris, with pictures of his designs for tapestries and textiles.

Note to parents and teachers
Every effort has been made by the Publishers to ensure that these websites are suitable for children. However, because of the nature of the Internet, it is impossible to guarantee that the contents of these sites will not be altered. We strongly advise that Internet access is supervised by a responsible adult.

Index